wing in the Supercomputer

North Alaska

To locate the environmental forecasts and data landscapes of the Unknown Fields city the studio travels to Alaska's far north, to visit a territory that sits in the collective imagination as one of the last remaining wildernesses. Here climate change is not a condition that is going to play out in a possible future but is a phenomenon unfolding in real time. Whale migration patterns are shifting, coastlines are disappearing, and the ice is melting. Unknown Fields spend the winter solstice with climate scientists from around the world who are camped out in the most northern cities on the planet to collect data that is fed into the climate-modelling supercomputers and environmental policies further south.

From the oracles and augurs of the ancients to the predictive modelling of modern digital prophets, through the ages both wise men and charlatans have claimed to see into the future. Cultures differ in their concept of time and their attitudes towards the future, which are central to these acts of prediction. Alaskan Inuit, informed by ancestral memories of their environment and its patterns, embrace the uncertainties of the future with a deep belief in their own ability to adapt. Meanwhile, the world's environmental scientists attempt to assemble their observations into climate models in order to predict the future as precisely as possible. Caught between improvisation and premeditation these cultural relationships with landscape and time will define the future of the North and in turn our cities beyond.

This book peers inside the supercomputer to find a set of surreal landscapes, ones that sit between tradition and technology, the real and the imagined, the present and the future. They are landscapes narrated by native Alaskan authors and generated from the climate data and modelling software of supercomputer scientists. Against these images run panoramas of the supercomputer infrastructure that simulates them and the doomsday statistics that are shouted at us everyday, but that we do our best to ignore. Traditional data visualisations and guilt-laden headlines are no longer sufficient strategies to encourage the cultural shift required. Unknown Fields crack open the black box to pull out the environments the supercomputer is predicting and imbue them with new narratives. The indigenous poetry is an alternative mythology for an ever melting landscape of fear and hope. Panoramas that are dramatisations of data, portraits of a world we may have already lost or one we are yet to find.

64°51'23.48"N
147°51'5.79"W

The path we'd followed faded and became the path we had to follow. Tiny Arctic plants bending out of the way, flattening themselves against the sod, kneeling to our need to pass, to keep moving even when the way changed. A trail, once trod, takes a long time to unreveal itself, to fill in, grow over, disappear. Some things still happen slowly.

Words by Alaskan Native Poet Priscilla Naungagiaq Hensley

The mountain range and low hills of the landscape are height-map terrains generated by inputting global CO2 emissions data.

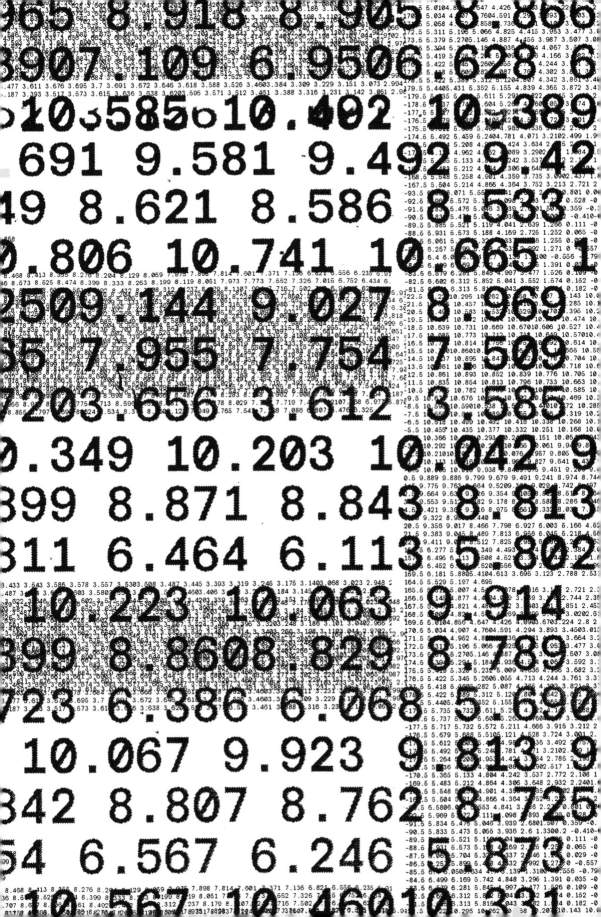

They lay beneath a giant, pale sky endlessly lit by a fading sun. Faces pressed against spiky tundra plants. Their eyes remained locked even as stems probed ears, cheeks, temples, pricking through, tasting their veins and, much like mosquito proboscises, splitting off to root in deeper. Nerve cells alight, afire with a stream of data drawn straight from the earth, their eyes overfilling with love and tears, everything from the smell of their mothers to the taste of berries and oil turned on like a river undammed. From deep below the surface came the pure song of blood long filtered through sod and fresh rain. The two, fingers intertwined, opened their mouths, singing in ones and zeros, bones and hearts; jacked in.

PNH

THE ⓩ⓪ WARMEST YEARS HAVE OCCURRED SINCE 1981 AND WITH ALL 10 OF THE WARMEST YEARS OCCURRING IN THE PAST 12 YEARS

64°51'23.48"N
147°51'5.79"W

When she was small, they'd dig a tiny siġluaq – cold storage – into slight hills of the tundra. Children's games, miniature life. They didn't have to dig deep to find the permafrost.

PNH

The now covered mountains are rendered from height-map terrains that have been generated by inputting mean temperatures collected by climate scientists from around the Arctic Circle.

IPCC FORECASTS A TEMPERATURE RISE OF 2.5 TO 10 DEGREES FAHRENHEIT OVER THE NEXT CENTURY

The drag hook of the mind asthenic
catches yet on green not so gone
though scrolled in absent a horizon
banked with clouds turning forth,

driven by wind. Let us set nostalgia
in a harness. A pathogen is drawn
upstream from metal culvert buckled
in sweet brook water under road again.

Let us see dust risen into light, subtracted
into rain. Our spring runs dry beneath
snow on a land now arid, now seams
of admonition: do not solve, adapt.

Words by Alaskan Native Poet Joan Naviyuk Kane

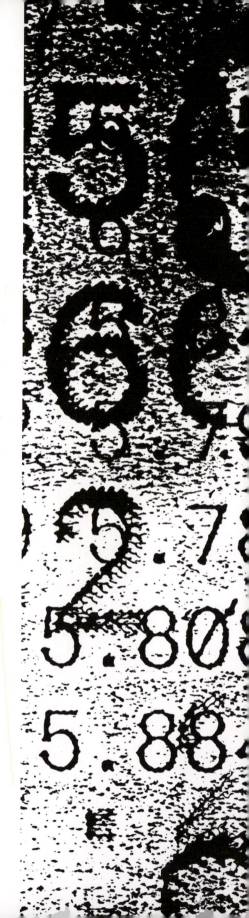

THE AREA OF THE PERENNIAL ICE HAS BEEN STEADILY DECREASING SINCE THE SATELLITE RECORD BEGAN IN 1979

64°51'23.48"N
147°51'5.79"W

Iuqpaktuk aqqataani.
Iuqpaktua.
Tavra kanŋuzukaluaqłuŋa tauq,

isaaq imam qaŋasaq.

Ice pressure ridges were forming all around us.
Pressure ridges were building with great
intensity.
I felt quite shy about it too,

from times long ago, beyond memory.

JNK

The strata of the exposed ice
walls in the landscape have
been encoded with the waveforms
of a soundscape generated by
listening to the data tapes
from the Fairbanks climate
supercomputer.

GREENLAND LOST 150 TO 250 CUBIC KILOMETRES OF ICE PER YEAR BETWEEN 2002 AND 2006

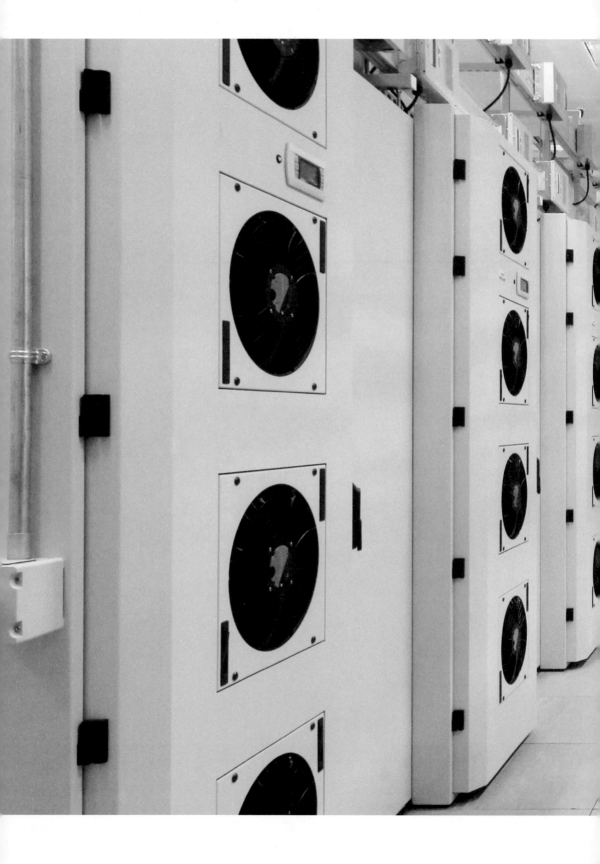

The skeletons assemble,
buried trade beads brought to light
gleam like ruin run glamorous alluvium:
evidence of someone else's way through valleys
dense, interior and distant.
I learn to long for thought arising through the
floor of my mind, a song alone in sound
recessed into the small noise of my breath.
The tongue turns –
It may be asked, why I insert
the mammoth, as if
it still existed? I ask in return
why I should omit…
I am little more than a string figure, one
of a divided couple danced into a seam of time.
At the margin of such desolation a relic so worn –
He may well exist there now,
as he did formerly where we find his bones.
The eye of a storm stares inward:
all fallen together, yours for excavation.

JNK

THE WARMEST INDIVIDUAL YEAR IN THE 160-YEAR MET OFFICE HADLEY CENTRE GLOBAL TEMPERATURE RECORD IS 2015 WITH A TEMPERATURE OF 0.44 ± 0.1°C ABOVE THE 1981—2010 MEAN

64°51'23.48"N
147°51'5.79"W

Gentle being, how do you float across the ice to me? You somehow know my heart's become overheated, that I churn, churn, churn, my own friction burning me up. I can only stand here on the edge again and look, wait, yearn. Fog rises. Strong being, you leap from pan to pan, something a child could do if we'd ever let one anymore. Somehow you know I need your courage. You burst through the mist, over and over again. I try to breathe you in.

PNH

The pink clouds floating above the ice field is a particle simulation that has been produced from a global carbon emissions data set.

97% ←

NINETY-SEVEN PERCENT OF CLIMATE SCIENTISTS AGREE THAT CLIMATE-WARMING TRENDS OVER THE PAST CENTURY ARE VERY LIKELY DUE TO HUMAN ACTIVITIES.

Wheel of the old thing
thrown out makes a cold
circuit. Three nights
ago an apparition

urged me to repent.
The city is his, it glisters.
I worried snow down
from the roof. It buried me.

A grid of lights gave way
to another body, thin relief
of land beneath
too little snow and no –

I have watched other
women twist their locks
into gleam and gloss
and have swallowed

a battery, passel, past.
Butane, propane
and lungful of diesel.
I did not stand a chance.

Always with poison
breath, bill, responsibility.
A man with rote hands.

Everything in exchange,
rain in a frozen season.
Our roof, roofs strung

with hot wire. Our love,
what was, an impression
of light, gaunt: there is

nothing to get.

JNK

NEAR RECORD TEMPERATURES ARE PREDICTED FOR THE COMING FIVE YEARS

64°51'23.48"N
147°51'5.79"W

I let him do what he will to me –
we are travelling into the waves
and the ocean is torn by swells.

I am cautious. The moon,
it can barely be sensed,
it cannot be helped.

I learned something, I am learning.
I am untangling a rope.
I am caught by a breaking wave.

The boat is rolling from side to side
I tell of my going to town –
what he threw broke through,

it has broken away.

JNK

The waveforms of a soundscape
generated by running a
Fairbanks supercomputer data
tape through a reel-to-reel
player have been used to form
a layer of cirrus clouds above
the churning ocean.

PROCEEDING AT A RATE THAT IS UNPRECEDENTED IN THE PAST 1300 YEARS

In the morning there came a new bird's call. It seemed louder than all the others either because it stood out or because the other birds were shocked into near silence. What is it saying? Where is it from and (perhaps more importantly) are there others on the way?

PNH

THE TOP 700 METERS OF OCEAN SHOW WARMING OF 0.302 DEGREES FAHRENHEIT SINCE 1969

64°51'23.48"N
147°51'5.79"W

Kiguàayak – the Aurora Borealis. *Auk* – blood.
Both plasmas.
Movement, matrices, mysteries.

PNH

The patterning of the landscape aurora has been simulated using a NASA analysis of global ocean current predictions.

THE GREENLAND ICE SHEET HAS BEEN LOSING AN ESTIMATED 287 GIGATONNES PER YEAR

ESKIMOS VISUALISE HELL AS A FINE PLACE TO LIVE.

JNK

64°51'23.48"N
147°51'5.79"W

It will be the water rising. Not just against the measure of shorelines and house posts, but as a needed, necessary thing. Fear fluttering in parched mouths. The journey will be long. It will seem novel, risky. It may be.

PNH

Texturing on the iceberg is generated from the translation of a projected global temperature rise data set into a three dimensional noise map.

Pale grass: vitiligo thrust from the tract
of his scalp, now mine. Your voice,

a sforzando of light as it strikes the rock-ridge
hung above the dwellings.

Or, your voice, a grim notation of the sweep
between us. All night along with you
our sons respire. I fever through memory.

The world that survives me is but a
dangerous place.

JNK

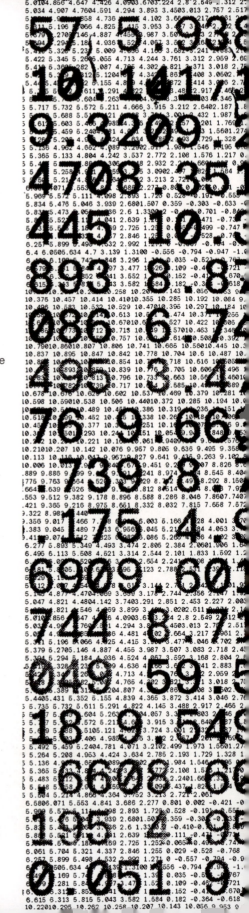

> **WORLD WILL HAVE EXCEEDED 2050 SAFE CARBON EMISSIONS LIMIT BY 2020**

64°51'23.48"N
147°51'5.79"W

It does not make much sense to mourn the things
I will never know
But that isn't stopping me from doing it.

Beyond that vast sea
are the things I don't even know I don't know.
And beneath that, the limitless blue-black galaxy
of what I'll never even come close to imagining.

One evening I was told a hunting story. They
walked on snowshoes around mountains. It only
took the old man five, six minutes to skin a
tuttu. Their tracks a distant white line and
it was seventy degrees below zero that night.

Sometimes, years ago, no one came back with food
and all the child had was lard and wandering
wishes skittering in the cold. Grownups eager
to push away from winter's camp.

I've already forgotten so much that was said.
Here is a little I remember.

You can leave a caribou with its feet poking up
and the ravens will leave it alone. Some people
like to make their *quaq* that way. The Inupiaq
words I'm so pleased my son uses are not even
fragments of our language. Shards is too sharp
and they're more happily and lovingly employed.
Bits is even too big. And they're small. So
small. Atoms, maybe.

I've heard people say they've forgotten more
than they know. We're standing here on an edge
with it all falling toward and away at the same
time. Feeling so much, like it's all just there
on the other side. Not enough falling through
me will catch. My blind eyes and dampened ears
will never know.

And so much is gone, gone.

PNH

The moonlit mountain range has been generated using the sound frequencies taken from an audio recording of the UK's most powerful climate supercomputer located at the Met Office.

Snowing in the Supercomputer by Unknown Fields

Design: Neasden Control Centre & City Edition Studio
Illustration: Neasden Control Centre

Printed in Italy by Musumeci S.p.a.
ISBN 978-1-907896-88-0

© 2016 Architectural Association and the Author

No part of this book may be reproduced in any manner whatsoever without written permission from the publisher, except in the context of reviews

For a catalogue of AA Publications visit
aaschool.ac.uk/publications or email publications@aaschool.ac.uk

AA Publications
36 Bedford Square
London
WC1B 3ES
t + 44 (0)20 7887 4021
f + 44 (0)20 7414 0783